MW01641147

songs for summer nights

poems

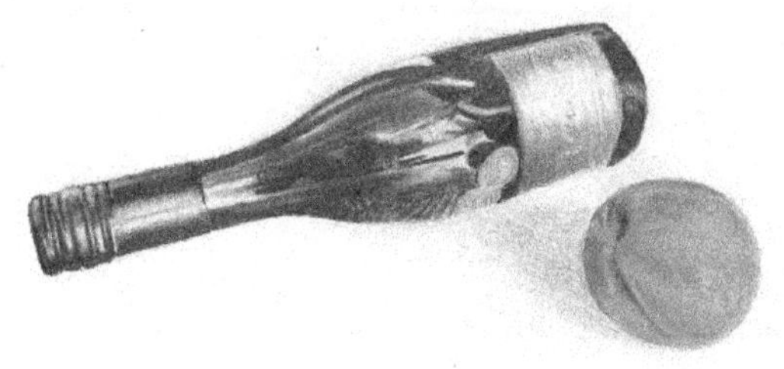

michael mahin || pumpkin boy press

songs for summer nights

Written by Michael Mahin.

Design by Michael Mahin.
Illustrations & Cover Design by Cat Beaudoin.
Logo by Skye Murie.

Published by Pumpkin Boy Press, Arlington, MA.

ISBN (trade paperback): 979-8-218-50946-0

Pumpkin Boy Press

• Website •
www.pumpkinboypress.com

• Instagram •
instagram.com/pumpkinboypress

• Facebook •
facebook.com/pumpkinboypress

for skye, for cat

c o n t e n t s

j u n e

j u l y

a u g u s t

j u n e

harvest moon

(neil young, 1992)

***

summer dream

(bonny light horseman, 2022)

***

the desperate kingdom of love

(pj harvey, 2004)

***

you and me

(penny & the quarters, 2007)

***

tell him

(lauryn hill, 1998)

***

bruises

(chairlift, 2008)

- untitled -

harvest moon
and white wine

tired after
the beach

dinner burnt
barely-touched

we were grimy
with seaweed

and saltwater

with sand
and dried sweat

and yet

we couldn't wait
to get to bed

to end this day
in the gentle throes

of arms
and drowsiness

heads pressed
against shoulders

legs tangled
like cords

hairs entwined
like braided rope

until we were
indistinguishable

just boy-on-boy
lazy-and-satiated

still, we waited
for a while

sitting quietly
in the ochre glow

of the porch light --
wishing, wanting

this day back
before it's even

really ended
yet

so we delayed
deferred

just listened
for the song

of cicadas
(their tired trill)

we even got naked
in each other's eyes

silently

before finally
cupping our hands

blowing out
the candles

and going back
inside

- participate -

as a kid --

in this dappled world
of light, through leaves,
and me, so silent in it

summer --

and watching the world
through a web of fingers,
a sort-of sieve for sunlight

fingers open,
and so suddenly light
and the like,
and the flowering trees
and skinned knees

fingers close,
and now i'm alone
with that warm,
orange semi-darkness,
which i seem to hold
in my hands

only

or perhaps
so often
somewhere
in-between

and i guess you could say
i sort-of spent
my whole life that way:

fingers close,
fingers open

the sounds of kids:
i'm open,
i'm open

and me,
just standing still,
palm to my face

and i guess you could say
i always really wanted it
both ways:

wanting to be known,
and yet
on-my-own

wanting to be alone,
and yet
not-alone

- june 21 -

2018 / post-chemo

i don't think i felt colors
again until that summer

the spring was slate,
steel gray, and dull

still, the robins came
quick and early, in the

mornings, in the trees,
bright-breasted, orange,

like the sun, and their song
such a strange salve of sorts:

sounding like warm bread,
and bathwater, and cups of tea,
with honey, and the nudging of wind
at bare knees, in those evenings spent outside
on my parents' porch, and drinking beer, bit buzzed,
smiling, some stevie song, inky-indigo sky, and near 11,
the neighborhood below a burnished, black-ish-blue, and
there's nothing to do, really, just the whipping wind and
an errant dog bark, amidst the dark, and the fleeting
spark of being 23-almost 24

///

so, i was good. i waited. i was patient.
sat, sipped my coffee, black, amidst
those stubborn icicles of april.

watched the sun move, shift, shine

weakly, shine better-brightly. trying.
and so i waited. and watched, as that

whole hazy, bitter season, bees tried
and tried mightily to ease smooth
honey out of cool, battered places.

(of which i knew -- i was one.)

i sat on my wind-rattled porch in
spring, in sleet, as soft and uncertain
as the day i arrived, day i was diagnosed.

i waited and waited and waited for
summer. and lived in the interim.
just let the days pass by, quietly die.

and so the bits of pale blue around the
edges of things slowly became teal,
became turquoise, became cobalt

and cornflower.

and the robbins sang, the sun grew and
i knew -- and then one day, in june or
maybe july, i realized -- it was summer

and i was alive, still had so much to live.
(i hoped). so much unknown, so much
of me to know, to grow.

and i wanted to.
and i do.
i do.
i do.
i do.

- where i go when i meditate -

soft sounds of the tv |
blaring from a distant room |
wizard of oz, maybe |
or *bringing up baby* |

and there's rain |
at the windowpane |
and a kettle quietly |
screaming somewhere |
and the house is impossibly warm |
and the house is gently rattled by wind |

but even so |
the sky is trying to smile |
and the light is almost there |
almost there |

and my grandmother's hands |
are in my hair |
and we're breathing softly |
circadian |
in rhythm |
not really talking |
don't need to |

and melly is there |
and now vicky too |
and they're smiling |
so i'm smiling too |

and this night is long |
and this night is good |
this night is never-ending |

and when i eventually open my eyes |

my room is always the same |
tv's off |
no impossible warmth |
or kettle |
or quiet howl of wind |
just silence |
dim light |
and incense |

but then i notice |
the way my head is almost-warm |
in that very place |
where my grandmother |
had stroked my hair |
mere moments ago |

as if we were really there |
in that place |
together |
because we were |
in a way |

because these things are real |
because these things happen |
or they will |
one day |

like that little bit of light |
left peeking |
through steel clouds |

or the sounds of the tv |
telling us it's time |
to go back to *oz* |
or maybe |
like all good things, really... |

always |
ultimately |
inevitably |
returning to us |

- plastic dinosaur -

for gagee

pulled me in real close,
and she whispered:

i have seen angels.

and i wasn't really sure
i knew what she meant.

but her eyes were like coals,
burning blackly, brightly.

and all around us that season
were sparrows and wilted grass.

the sun on our back porch,
dark lines slanting across

sun-bleached white wood --
all of it looking so good

so pure, i couldn't really
put a finger on what i felt.

hugging the plastic dinosaur
to my chest, as she leaned in,

and kissed my ear
with her secret.

so all i really knew

was how hushed she was
in shades of purple,

how much i wanted
to be the thing that

shone in her eye,
and how the wind reminded me

of how much i loved her.

///

so sometimes, i think
about going back to that day,

and in the fantasy:

putting the plastic dinosaur
back in my hand,

stringing the summer sun
back up in the sky,

placing the inky glimmer
back in her eye,

so that i could nod, facing her,
but then this time i'd whisper:

me too.

and i still do.

- lemons -

every day,

he fills the basin of his gladness
with things seen but rarely or barely noticed:

// the softly trembling hands of a stranger //
// the green and whispering trees //
// the bright yellow lemons in the bowl //

again and again,
he makes himself see,
until he forgoes, forgets,
what made him forget them

in the first place

- porch chair (*haiku*) -

i have felt god here
she is the wind wrapped around
my toes, the s t a r k sun

- in rest, you awaken your life -

there were so many blades
of grass that summer –
silent summer

curtains drawn,
windows of the houses dark
mid-day, monday

so warm, sleepy
in those streets
always wandering

and i bent down to peer
into my own shadow
just a dark imprint

on pavement

sidewalk, walking home
or sometimes
far from home

and i'll admit:

i was a little like
a phantom
in those days

but alive and attuned
to the smell of garden phlox
and dianthus

the glare of the summer sun,
the sounds of sprinklers on lawns
like the soft hissing of snakes

but languid, lazy
(i was that, too)

frittered away days
in the gentle buzz
of being alive

sat by empty churches
fingering the pages of books
i had always wanted to read

fell asleep in porch chairs,
just sort-of drifted off
in the middle of the day

and i felt my body hum
with the hunger of rest
and wanting m o r e

walked off a sadness
i thought might always last,
outlast me

wondered if i could
outrun it,
out-rest it

and, still,
like the sun or a stray,
the sadness came back

but, then again,
as you may have guessed,

this isn't really the point

- real -

| | when does life get real? | |

after they removed the port,
after the pandemic ends,
after this steel cloud of depression dissipates,
after the degree, and the dog,
and the house, and the houseplant,
the happy hubby,
the pictures on the mantle, smiling,
the fireplace, flames crackling?

after i have sleeves,
have covered my body in ink?

after 5 years out,
after my mother's second tattoo, to commemorate,
after the pink of the port scar
no longer catches my breath,
catches me in a cold sweat,
after the lack of sun stops hurting,
after the buzz of being good wears off,
after the last gasp of wanting everyone, anyone,
to like me?

after this swim,
after this song,
after this car ride with my mother,
who glances in the rearview mirror,
sighs, and then says, almost off-handedly:

i feel like i've lost touch with my life.

which spooks me, really,
because i know exactly
what she means.

and so i ask, in earnest:

how do you get back,
you know... in touch?

and she laughs, pauses, then says --
serious, sincere, all-of-a-sudden:

when you figure that out, let me know...
will you?

- 9-to-5 -

i will always want this –

my body, weightless in water.
and music. and iced coffee.

day free of the me
that needs to prove

that i work hard,
that my value is quantifiable.

that it can be measured
in sleeplessness, overtime,

dollar amount and/or
gold star on the chart.

give that gold star away.

that thing won't prove
you're curious, or kind,

or in touch with yourself.

you won't be able to take
it with you to the grave.

and so when i'm dead
and gone, let them say:

he was kind,
loved fiercely,
laughed a lot,
and enjoyed his life.

- coffee shop -

at kickstand cafe

sometimes the light is just right.
sometimes i sit and stare at things.

summer, the scent of grass,
and some song that feels like it lives
inside my bones.

kickstand, coffee, and the day ahead
unfurling so sort-of slow.

i don't know,
these are small things, i suppose.

and yet --
and yet --

this is why i'm here.
my breath is in this.
my blood is in this,
too.

sometimes it feels like
i choose to be happy.

over and over again,
i make the choice,
daily.

(however hard)

i sit in the light.
i let it lick my wounds.

it doesn't take the wounds away --
can't color every darkened day.

and yet --
and yet --
and yet --
and yet --

- affogato -

i read about this dish, in italy --

you take a scoop of pearly-white,
milk-flavored gelato
and then pour piping-hot espresso,
or *caffettiera*, on top

patiently waiting
as the scorched-earth torrent of espresso
envelops the sweetly cold gelato

which, in turn, proceeds to
m
e
l

t
with the sudden intrusion (explosion!)
of bitter-black heat.

they say the gelato
should essentially be "drowned" in it --
the espresso, i mean.

///

one day, i would very much
like to sit in a cafe
somewhere in italy --

alone, though not lonely –
or, at the very least, not very --
at some small, tucked-away table,
which i've commandeered
for the afternoon,

books, and papers, and cups
and cups of now-tepid coffee,
plates stacked up in front of me,
formerly-full, since-licked-clean

nowhere to be,
not ready to leave

and watch and relish
the way that opal-white
stone-cold-as-ice gelato
is drowned in its bitter enemy.

nearly demolished, destroyed --
yet, instead, tasting even better
than you had first believed --

a little bit bitter

and yet

somehow –

somehow –

still sweet.

- seagull at the edge of the world -

june 2018 / post-chemo

we watched the waves lap, erode,
the algae-dusted rocks and stones
below.

the beach was deserted,
the wind a frigid howl,
the sky an ashen blue.

a seagull cried from nearby,
once, twice, and then
just sand and silence.

its webbed feet were planted, perched,
territorially, in a tangle of dried seaweed.

i watched its beady little eye,
black as coal,
dart to and fro,
searchingly.

and i smiled.
i was cold.
i was happy to be there.

it felt a little like the edge of the world.
the day was odd, almost-over.

hushed, mid-day, weekday.
everyone at work,
except for us.

i ran my hand over my head,
ghost spot of where my hair

once used to be.

now just thin stalks of brown,
coming in quietly.

i looked at my father, whose face
suddenly looked so much like my own,

and asked:

where to now?

and he looked at me,
i mean really looked at me,
cleared his throat, and said:

i don't know.

and then:

anywhere you want.

- night swimming -

for j and a

tequila, gold -- killed the bottle,
watched the sun rise in shades
of pink and periwinkle

it was a time --
it was a time --

and zipping down darkened roads --
we listened to *the psychedelic furs*
and "love my way" on a loop

at the diner the morning after --
the waitress eying us skeptically,
like dirty dishrags, things to be

disposed, suspicious of --
handed us cups of lukewarm coffee,
her stencil eyebrow arched

we wore paper hats,
asked for a picture, solicitous,
and so she sighed, obliged,

none-too-happy -- and in the picture,
we look mummified, miserable,
but we weren't really

we were happy --
we were happy --

placed all of the terror of our twenties
into one weekend, into the bottle --
and killed it

it was a time --
it was a time --

then, later, night swimming,
skinny dipping, under the stars,
a dark sparkle in the sky,

and i... *shit --*

i was happy --
i was happy

- white wine / black garden ant -

the day was confetti:

glittering and good,
already gone.

i traced, with my thumb,
the nape of your neck,
still slick with sweat.

then i spotted,
among the tufts
of bright, surprising green,

the discarded heads
of strawberries,

which were blood-red
and sweet.

and the empty wine glass,
which was lying sideways
in the grass.

and there were ants
crawling up inside
its curved lip,
delicate.

i watched their hungry
scuttling, search,
their gleaming
black bodies,

and was happy
as i thought
quite suddenly:

yes,
they do, they do

they deserve
such sweetness   too.

- two-men-in-a-bed-love-song -

for g

outside your window
i could hear a black-capped chickadee
singing

early morning

and the tug of wind
and rustling leaves
and the dazed rushing of cars
and eventually church bells

my body was pressed, nested, inside yours
one hand wrapped around your chest
the other gently stroking your hair

i stared at the dotted, milky, imperfect
expanse of your back
which was beautiful

listened as you groaned faintly
half-asleep, half-happy
not an actual admission
of pacification or pleasure
(probably)

though even still
i liked to think it was

maybe if only because
in that white morning light
in which you looked
so very handsome

i suddenly realized what all
those songs and poems --

including the ones
i, myself, had written, once
back when i knew nothing --

had been about
all this time

- it's june, we're faggots, and the world still hates us -

half-quietly,
half-hatefully.

yes --
even the corporations that *love* us.

we swish, and sway,
and laugh too loud,
or not at all.

and if the men's eyes --
on the train,
on the bus,
in the crowded bars,
or the corner stores --
were knives,
we would have,
should have,
died already

but we didn't.

instead,
we kissed.

- cape cod -

there is an easy silence
in that space between us

it lives in cafe corners
and cups of hot coffee

it is even in the air
in cape cod

where we were wild
and wet for days

with sweat
and saltwater

and, yes, okay
i remember our feet
tangling together

but more than that:
i remember your smile
and silence

and walking wordlessly
over stone and sand
along a private beach

where we just ambled
along all afternoon,

not-really-awkward
just quietly content

and afterwards
dinner on the back porch

of your friend's summer home

where we were more-or-less
squatting for the weekend

and the wine was almost warm
(from sitting out all afternoon)

and the salad was sparse
and overdressed

but i didn't care

and i watched the way
you were so sort-of gorgeous
in the glare

of the porch light
(so sweetly sienna)

i almost didn't want
to break the spell
with words

so that later,
when you asked:

do you think you've ever
felt a bit of the real thing?

i paused for a moment
before i looked you
in the eye and said:

i have

j u l y

still in love

(cat power, 1996)

***

lover's spit

(broken social scene, 2002)

***

the one to wait

(ccfx, 2017)

***

victim of love

(charles bradley, 2013)

***

wish i was

(kim deal, 2013)

***

lean into life

(petey, 2021)

- july 1 -

we fell into it in june:

the late-day light, the grocery list.
the milk in the fridge gone off.
the boy in the bar who flirts with you, in front of me.
the white wine, the red wine. gin.
your friends. the drunken dinner parties.
the solicitous half-smiles, the happy-host.
playing the part (i wanted them to like me).
the burglar, the vanishing laptop.
the changing locks, changing weather.
the summer storms, the nights full of lightning.
the shifting sand-beneath-feet.
the bad birthday dinner.
the weekends at the cape.
the board games, the buzz, the early nights in.
the water in your eyes as you say something.
the tug, telling me: *you will not get to love this for very long.*
the time i catch you in a lie. catch you in a cold-sweat.
the early morning light, alone.
the empty side of the bed. the indent.
the quiet before you cough, then say, *hey, can we talk?*
and your voice is tense, taut, as wire.
the way i couldn't even move my mouth to say some
small, likely-stupid thing.
the dust dancing mid-air, through shafts of sunlight.
the brick, the back bay window, wednesday, so bright.
and in the light, you look sorta beautiful,
like how i remember you, from that december
when we met, hands frigid over ice-cold beers,
outside, 30-some-odd-degrees. and i didn't, couldn't,
know whether this would become something,
but i liked the bright in your eyes, dimples,
your snaggletooth.
i liked you, wanted you, wanted you to want me too.

30 degrees and, still, i said something like: *i feel sorta warm*,
then went maroon. and you did too.
even though i wasn't really sure whether you meant to.
or were just trying to be nice.
always afraid of that, because i was like that.
waiting for the other shoe to drop -- but i was the shoe.
afraid it was you.
always watching as some softly beautiful boy blanched,
then sighed, watching the water in my eyes.
knew what was coming.
always already-ready to be alone.
that is, until you.
and… fuck.
and then the changing air, changing breath,
the light in your eyes gone for good. gone for me (good
for someone else, i guess).
the end arriving quietly, the click of the lock, the ticking
of the clock as you left.
the sounds of city sirens outside.

the onset of july.

- saltwater -

i wanna be groggy, sunsick
in the passenger seat of your car

my head heavy and hung low
from the heat and sleeplessness

but feeling happy

how the downtown strip
smelled of saltwater, sea

and fried fish

your fingers cradling my hip
and the beads of sweat

running in rivulets
down your neck

or the way i was a bit more than buzzed
stumbling out of that seafood restaurant

after lunch

stepping out onto the street
and the sun suddenly felt so strong

like a slap
and you felt *so strong*

and i remember my hand
on your back, stabilizing

but really,

i just wanted to be close to you
an excuse

the way we both smelled of beer
or how i nearly felt you up in the partition

by the hostess stand
in that boat-themed bar

we both hated

your crooked smile
as my normally shy hands

then went wandering
roguishly, impolitely

in public

you laughed and i laughed
and the hostess hated us

(i didn't blame her)

and the drinks were watery
pretentious, overpriced

but you said:
you pay for the view

and i remember watching you
and the light reflecting off the water

the sound of the waves lapping
against the rocks below, intermingling

with that midday summer silence

and you were handsome
the day was humid

my head felt hazy

so all i wanted was your tongue
the sound of sea foam melting

or a song on the stereo after
the long drive home

(fleetwood mac)

or in the parking lot outside
that dilapidated ice cream shop

and milkshakes and music blaring
and the car was so fucking hot

i though we might explode

and i wanted you, i mean
r e a l l y wanted you

and we couldn't wait
didn't want to

and so we went there

in the blistering air
of the car cabin

hoping no one would see
but we didn't really care

and i remember you were warm
in my mouth

and i never got the stains out
of that pj harvey t-shirt

but i didn't care
i wore it all day,

anyway

and okay, so i was drunk
but i was happy too

so sometimes i still wonder:

do you wish you'd been spared
the trip, or the trouble, or the way
i dragged my lips across yours
behind the bar, like i was writing
my name in your mouth
kissing you with consonants?
do you wish you could take it back
because it didn't last?
i know the buzz wears off
but i was happy
(really happy)
in that moment
and you did that.

do you ever think about that day?
did i do that for you, too?

i don't know
but i really hope so.

- hanover st, boston, july -

you said:
i am a river

and i smiled,
laughed,
pushing the empty plate
away from me,
replied:
okay, you're drunk

and you said:
no, really, listen--

and raised your hand,
as if to pause
the sweltering summer air

to stop the symphony
of city traffic sounding
behind us

and suddenly the world,
the buzzed and bustling street,
hanover street,
north end,
boston

everything was silent

every gesture frozen, mid-air,
every face but yours
unmoving

and i leaned in
to listen

and, quite miraculously,
could hear the babble
of cold water
rushing over rocks

and the river
of your body
running

always
running
towards me

(hopefully)

- blue moon (*haiku*) -

blue moon, a boy's bed
i choose to find holiness
anywhere i can

- peach -

macerated peaches
and red wine

the day had been
l o n g

slow-boil and
sticky

i placed my head
plum in the ice box

just for the icy thrum
soft slap, delicious blast

of cold, crisp air

you watched me, smiling
then said:

you know, if you aren't careful,
your face might freeze like that

and i laughed a little
in spite of myself

we had spent that whole day
inside

ceiling fan spinning
ceaselessly

but then the night cooled off
leaving a randy blue nip in the air

upstairs porch, summer-dusk
a breeze nuzzling at bare feet

as we watched the sunlight
bleed out over the horizon

in hues of deflated rouge
and muddy orange streaks

and so the white wine
followed the red

the bright yellow peaches,
with cream, were sweet

you said:
but you should always add a pinch of salt

and i nodded
said i knew what you meant

though i didn't, really
just trusted you, i guess

didn't feel the need
to defend the day

which was languid and happy
or myself in it

there are moments like that
(they're rare but they're there)

so, you took a sip from your glass
leaned back in your chair

asked:
are you getting cold?

your eyes warm
like the fire

but i said:
no, i'm fine

and you nodded
didn't need to ask again

and i think i must have
looked so gently happy

because the look in your eye
was perfect

a bit bittersweet
watching me for a while

before you finally said,
with a certain twinge:

careful, or your face
will freeze like that

- espresso -

he made me an espresso
after.

we lounged in the post-sex silence
eating chocolate biscotti

in the sun-filled living room
which had a view of the ocean

from every window, every angle
just wide-water-blue

and the shimmer, sheen
of mid-day, white light

coating everything.

my hair was mussed, messy
from his hands

which had been
everywhere on me

mere moments ago.

i thought about the way
he had said my name

as he came

a guttural exclamation
of me:

michael!

so, i sipped the dark espresso slowly
just sort-of looking around.

his house was quite beautiful --
the kind you usually see on tv

or in catalogs.

the kind i knew i would never own
on my own.

we chatted lightly, mostly
dancing around the words

already bandied about, wordlessly
body-to-body, in the bedroom

before.

he was kind-of kind and married
asked to take a photo of me

grinning softly, clarifying --
to send to my hubby --

who was away for the weekend
but would have approved

he assured me.

and though i had felt sweetly sexy
for a small time, face-down

in this stranger's bed

i was also keenly aware that i was
a kind-of convenient

g h o s t

in his immaculate home
his otherwise-settled life.

because even as i was taking
his fingers into my mouth

i couldn't help but think
of his husband, briefly

who, i was almost sure,
didn't care that i was there

which made me lonelier
somehow.

and then i thought of you
as i do --

oh, i don't know --
about 1,000,001 times a day.

especially at the door
on my way out

when he asked me, off-handedly:
how is someone like you single?

and i smiled, laughed politely
before quickly exiting,

slipping into my car, exhaling,
peeling away from the curb,

fast –

just a blur of sudden
          surviving motion

and the rushing of wind
          through the car window

and the scream of the stereo
          the ocean, the roiling waves

the thrum of his breath in my ear
          the hum of the espresso machine

and your voice
          always your voice

          (*hello gorgeous*)

still ringing, ringing
          r i n g i n g in my ears.

- david -

sometimes,
            in the still morning,
i let that streak of light
            through my window
fall upon the mottled,
            milky place
inside my naked thigh
            i don't know why

and sometimes,
            at night, in bed,
i imagine myself much
            like the statue of david
just cut-white
            and perfect curvature
this sensual thing

            because yes,
i have had the body,
            i have been the body,
as the thing to suck,
            to fuck, to place down low,
on the hardwood,
            as if in a form of prayer,
or worship, or pure want,
            just an endless stream
of *more-moremoremoremore*

            have been the thing
to help us both forget
            for a minute,
to beat into the headboard,
            or to pretend to caress,

but then again:

what about the idea
of the body as a boat?
beautiful and battered
by so many storms?

as the thing
of such sensuous, uncertain,
imperfect, constant

carrying?

- tattoo you -

wading in, weightless,
water was pale green,
murky, wrapped
around my waist.

i knew,
even as i stood,
feet sinking further
down, down, *down*
into the muck,
that very likely
the older couple
on the beach
could see me --
all awkward angles
and pale-chested.

my body
as the curious canvas.
the thing with ink.

so, without even
having to turn around,
i could imagine
her furrowed brow
and frown,
slight head tilt
and shake,
wondering:

jesus christ,
what was he thinking?

but then,
a beam of light

fell over the lake,
a gentle spotlight
slanting across,
warming, illuminating,
the right side
of my body.

which is where
i got my first tattoo.
when i was twenty.

weird year,
just wanted to mark it
somehow.
one-and-done.

but then there have been
many weird years since.

and so yes, i guess
you could say
that i have been in a battle
with my body
since the day we met.

so i wish
i could make
the woman
with the white hair
and glare,
or her similarly
sullen husband,
understand.

what it's like to like
the feeling of furrowing
ink into flesh.

to turn
the brokenness
of this body
into something
beautiful,
my serrated edges.

a sort-of prayer
for the power of
something
you love so deeply,
you want it
inside you
(forever).

the beating
of song into skin.
lyric into ligament.
blue into bones.

i think joni
said it best:

(blue) songs are like tattoos

and i've spent
my whole life
marking their melodies
in me

with the nudging
of needles
and grace
of an (ink) gun –

the only one i trust.

my body of
blue songs
& bar songs
& sad songs
& scar songs.

my body of
love songs.

- little one / ladybug -

i wish i knew what i was
already

yesterday,
walking through the city,
a man stopped me,
asked if i was married
or had kids
(in spanish)

i shook my head
and he just smiled
back at me
sadly

yesterday,
i walked by the ocean
for the thousandth time
this month

i didn't stop to marvel
at its cerulean surface
or the glistening,
granular sand

just really needed to get out
of the apartment,
i guess

yesterday,
i worked, and watched,
and waited, and wanted,
and smiled falsely,
and laughed at the right times
and was lonely,

and then went to bed
early

yesterday,
i watched a wayward ladybug
on the white tile wall
of my cramped shower,
trying mightily
not to get wet,
to avoid the torrent
of rushing water

i picked it up gently,
with my forefinger,
inspected its round,
red body, smudged,
dotted with black,

and then, before placing it
outside my bathroom window,
whispered:

you're lost,
little one,
but just for now,
not forever

and then
let it go
off, out
into the world

sailing in uncertainty
towards what
i hoped was something,
somewhere
like home.

- ecdysis -

i get low in the evenings
when the body is meant to relax,
to unwind,
unspool like the coiling rope

sloughing off the stress
around one's neck
like a second skin
// ecdysis //

instead, it is a cloud
i try to keep my head above
most days

nebulous,   nefarious
overworked,   underworked
            and anxious

and i don't know
if the sun is a cure,   really,
but i was sitting under its fuzzy glow
the other day when i realized
for about the thousandth time:

you are not the anxiety-riddled,
vaguely-evil thing you made up
in your mind

you can just sit here,
feet gently pricked by the plankwood,
watching the neighborhood below

its everyday green and breeze,
and wish to smile
until you do

for you were meant to do this,   too
for you were put here to do this,   too

- seventeen / cerulean -

january 2022, remembering how

there were days of trees & no traffic,
wind howling through open windows,
insistent-whisper of cars passing,
and laughter, music louder back then,
so much LOUDER

smoke in the park, the playgrounds
a sort-of hazy-yellow-glow, halos of light
from the drooping streetlights, and puddles,
petroleum, ink-black glassy -- and the streets
were slick, wet, recent-rain, the pitter-patter
on pavement, chalk-stained, running in rivulets
of color, muddy, right down to the gutter

or

a song of screaming heads from cars,
and stars, the night sky, driving just to drive,
just to be somewhere, anywhere -- didn't care,
or it didn't matter, in those days, really
just wanting the warmth of headlights,
red light (running it-gunning it),
used to do that, yeah,
we used to do that

sucking down lemon, neon-blue
syrup over crushed ice, smirnoff,
the jumbo-sized plastic cup,
and red straw, liberal sips/swigs,
still we winced, every time, and
the bitter pill, bitter buzz of being
seventeen, uncertain, serotonin
(and fuck -- i miss it)

howl of wind, howl of youth,
howl of something softer than this time
(*i hate it*), seventeen and missing nothing,
with only everything ahead, for nothing
has really happened yet, and yet --
everything is happening --

and so,
i still see trees and green leaves
passing from cars, and stars,
and feel buzzed on summer nights,
sometimes

but i wish i could tell you what it meant
back then -- to feel the wind coursing
through my hair, my head hanging out
the window of some faded red ford:
i was fresh-faced, freckled,
acne-scarred-already,
terrified and alive, seventeen

wishing for nothing --
~~(scratch that)~~
wishing for everything

because back then:

i used to touch things -- (*everything*)
i used to dream in blue -- (*cerulean*)
i used to put my head out the window and scream at
passersby -- (*because i could*)
because i wanted them to know, needed to remind
myself that -- (*i was alive*)

and so, fuck, i --
i guess i just miss it,
sometimes

- iced tea -

there's a sun
in the july sky
i do not recognize

the pale purple angelonia
bend towards the earth
as if in prayer

or perhaps
they're grieving

i touch their stems gently,
whisper:

yeah, me too.

as if they can hear me
(and perhaps they can)

the young woman
working the register
at the corner store
sighs, barely smiles

as i place the gum,
the arizona iced tea,
on the vinyl counter

tiny, empty things
i don't really need

just some small,
tangible reminder
that i am, in fact,
alive

the store is deserted,
the low groan from the ac,
the radio playing softly,
the hum of the refrigerators,
all such lonely sounds

the clerk brushes the dark,
dyed hair from her face,
glitter-black nail polish
and stick-n-poke tattoos,

and is about to sigh, again,
but then catches my eye,
its lowly look, my face
a subtle map of misery

and pauses, watching me,
then scans the gum,
the iced tea, deliberately
and places them
in the plastic bag

she handles both items
as if they're mementos,
keepsakes, so very sacred

and, after reporting
that'll be $2.99,
smiles at me softly,
sadly, sweetly

and i don't even know
how to return
this small gesture,
at this time in my life,
without it killing me --

so i simply nod,
and collect my change,
scooping the errant coins
into the palm of my hand
from the edge of the counter

and then, a moment later,
as i'm almost out the door,
almost out of earshot
(though not yet),
i can hear her whisper:

yeah, me too.

even though, in truth,
i haven't said anything

though perhaps i have

- tangerine -

for the friends who make us feel alive

martha peeled the orange with her teeth,
bare-feet, tangerine-smile, grinning in color

the apartment was small -- we used to sit on
the floor to watch daytime TV and talk shit

summer sunlight, and those grimy windows
were green with bright leaves -- plant-mom,

record sleeves everywhere -- *the vinyl ocean,*
is what we used to called it -- grace jones &

janis & joni & janet & stevie & solange &
sza & pj & patti & prince & all the others

our phonographic friends

we used to pass that cig like a burning bible,
a kind-of holy hand grenade to our lungs,

wine-teeth, stained-red, bed-head and dead-
tired, in our twenties -- i even remember the

way she used to smile -- chipped-tooth (two,
actually) and dimples, freckled and funny --

and how

she coughed a bit before she said something,
like -- *i love this* or *i get sorta low, sometimes* --

looked away, or glanced down at her hands,
picked the lint from her shirt, and always

avoided my eye, though i don't know why,
because we were the same, really, her & i

or maybe i do

know -- because we were afraid, weren't
really sure what to say, nervous it would

all go away in a flash: this temporary peace,
momentary magic, this quiet stalemate

with life -- we just wanted these moments
to mean something, wanted them never-

ending, because in them it felt like enough,
or okay, to simply be alive, with one another

just this --

smoke in the air and eating tangerines with the
TV on, curled up in that shifting patch of sun

smiling at each other through blazing orange
(peels) – and she laughed once, then got quiet

all-of-a-sudden and said, with this certain air of
sincerity and seriousness, black light in her eyes:

sometimes, i forget how much i miss my life, you
know, until i'm here, right here, eating tangerines
with you. -- (pause) -- *do you know what i mean?*

- blood moon dreaming -

i wanna dance, with all of my friends,
in a summer field, under a blood moon

bleary-eyed, buzzed, feverish with happy

i wanna throw my hands around so many necks,
sweaty and saying things i've always wanted to say

i love you in ways i can't contain, can't describe
i get so lonely sometimes, do you get that way too?

to the thrum, the insistence of disco,
and the lights, and the heat, and everything is perfect

and all of our sins are finally forgiven
and all the mistakes i've made aren't actually mistakes,
anymore

and every man i ever sort-of loved is standing there,
waist-high in the tall grass, smiling, wishing me well

and the me at 23 is there too, at the edge of the field,
watching, pale and boyish and bright-eyed

and as i near on him, i lean in to kiss him
and he kisses me back like he means it

then nods and just sort-of drifts away
into the softly whooping crowd

and for once,
i don't want or need to find him, to pin him down,

to strip off my clothes, put on his own --
instead, i just let him go

(let him go)

because i'm happy to be here --
in this very present moment,

in a summer field,
with all of my friends,
under a blood moon

- magnolia (1999) -

to the tune of "wish i was" by kim deal

***

"i don't know where to
put things, you know?"
-- quiz kid donnie smith, *magnolia* (1999)

***

i take my body to the bar,
to the boy in the bar,

to the bathroom fluorescents,

to the cold glass,
to the whiskey on ice,

to the hand which passes it,
to the man whose hand it is,

to the river of sheets,
to the river of sheets,

to the river,
to the frigid foam of the water,

to the woods,
to the trees which are green,
which are swaying, gently,

to the beach,
to the crystalline sand,

to the sullen street, at dusk,
to the silence of it,

to the car,
to the open window,

to the wind,
which is screaming,

to the hair,
which is whipping,

to the radio,
to the feral sound,

to the song of stevie,
to the scream of stevie,

to the laptop screen,
to the cups of coffee,

and the cups of coffee,
and the cups of coffee,

to the bed,
to the bar,

to the boy in the bar,
to the one who is smiling,

to the bathroom fluorescents,

to the grime of the mirror,
to the muddy reflection,

to the glass,
to the liquor

going *down-down-down*
the hatch,

to the salt
on the rim of the glass,

to the salt
on the back of one's hand,

to the lime,
which is sour,
which is green,

which one has to suck,
like poison,

between teeth,

to the man who watches,
then laughs,

to the slap of his hand
on my back,

to the slap of his hand
on my ass,

to the river of sheets,
to the river of sheets,

to the sweat,
to the spit in his hand,

to the hunger,
to the gasp as we inhale,

to the nitrites,
to the nights-like-this,

to the aftertaste,
to the always-alone

which comes-after-this,

to the dark of the street,
to the car which is parked,

to the bar,
to the boy in the bar,

to the bathroom fluorescents,

to the grime of the mirror,
to the bleary-eyed image of me,

to the ruddy complexion,
to the one i can't recognize,

to the dark of the road,
to my childhood home,

to the porch light,
to the stairs which precede it,

to my mother,
to the foot of her bed,

to the eyes which are mine,
which are red,

in the bathroom fluorescents,

to the pulse of the club,
to the pulse of this song,

to the *thump-thump-thump*,
to the confetti which rains,

to the bodies,
which are beautiful,

which are not like mine,
which are just like mine,

which are aching,

to the pink of the port scar,
which is aching,

to the drippppp of the iv,
to the *pop!* of the prednisone
taken,

going *down-down-down*
the hatch,

to the plush, pale gray
of the infusion chair,

to the hands of the nurse,
which didn't hold me,
yet still held me,

to the paleness of the body,
when it's shaken,

like the rattling of wind,
through leaves, through trees,

to the far-awayness of stars,
to the car, which is running,

to the open window,
to the blaring radio,

to the passing wind,
which is hurrying,
which has nowhere to be,

to the glow of the headlight,
to the yellow-now-red light,

to the nights full of song,
to the feral sound,

to the weed,
to the white wine,

to the *tick!* of the clock,
to the new tattoo,

to the pen which is buzzing,
to the blood and ink mixing,

to the hand which wipes the ink,
to the man whose hand it is,

to the sting of the needle,
to the red of the skin,

which is inflamed,
yet is healing,

to the sleeplessness,
to the appearance of the room,
at dawn,

to the always-returning-restlessness,
to the buzz of the body,

when it's lonely,
when it's aching,

to the river of sheets,
to the river of sheets,

to the salt on the rim,
to the salt on my fingers,

after he's finished,

to the slap of skin against skin,
against skin,

against skin,

to the bar,
to the drink,

to the glass,
to the whiskey on ice,

to the hand which passes it,
to the man whose hand it is,

to the light in his eyes,
to his wry smile,

which i love,
unquestionably,

to the wondrous way
you can feel still held by something,

even when gentleness
feels impossible, unreachable,

has for so long,

much like the sun,
like the far-awayness of stars,

but there it is, again:
gentleness

and this even after he fucks me,
in the car which is parked,

on the street,
which is empty,

the street,
which is lonely,

to the body which is aching,
which is mine,

to the warmth
creeping up my spine,

to the way he whispers my name,
like it means something,

to the beauty of his body,
that nest i couldn't fit in,

to the beauty of my body,
that nest i'm still burning,

or learning to burn,

like the phoenix,
which sets fire to its own nest,

doesn't it? because i swear
i heard that somewhere

i find myself saying aloud,
to no one, or maybe only to myself,

in the bathroom fluorescents

okay, okay, but then...
where do i put it??

i blurted out, later,
after he had let me down gently,

my voice shaky
with that decades-old desperation --

but he only stared at me,
the question bright in his eyes,

and so i said:

i mean my body.
i mean, shit -- i keep trying to find places to put my body.
just tell me where to put my body.

even though i don't think i only meant my body.

- in the dream -

all the cats have come back.
the river is no longer brown from the rust.

cells sit quietly,
stay in their place.

the body is the thing that bends,
doesn't break.

and the way the light catches the leaves,
in deep, deep summer -- it stays that way.

yellow, burnt white. and green.

and john puts down the bottle.
caitlin too.

the dead stand around your bed,
like a choir,
all bright, white light and wings.

softly singing your name.

and someone, somewhere, stops.
someone, somewhere else, says

sorry.

and nothing hurts.
nothing matters too-much,
or not-enough.

the sun is always softly certain,
before setting.

the record player spins endlessly,
stevie's voice waltzing in,
lighting every candle in the room.

and that bar is always open
for another hour.

your friends are always there.

the music throbs,
confetti rains,
the lights pulse like a fist.
and your mouth isn’t dry.
it isn't too late.

the air in the room feels
so full of everything –

wide-open and wild electricity
r u n n i n g
drenched in sweat.

and everyone is singing along
to some song that is as loud,
as thunderous,
as the voice of god.

the moment is now --
here, forever and present,
and future-tense,
all at once.

and the room isn’t even spinning yet,
even as you are --

spinning,
spinning,

spinning,
spinning
spinning
s   p
        I   N n
                        I   N g

just the whir,
the wonder,
the luxury
of motion,

never worried about
wasting a single breath,

never even looking
to get saved.

a u g u s t

sara

(fleetwood mac, 1979)

***

every time the sun comes up

(sharon van etten, 2014)

***

a song for our grandfathers

(future islands, 2014)

***

halcyon and on and on

(orbital, 1993)

***

ode to dance floor

(niki & the dove, 2016)

***

color song

(maggie rogers, 2017)

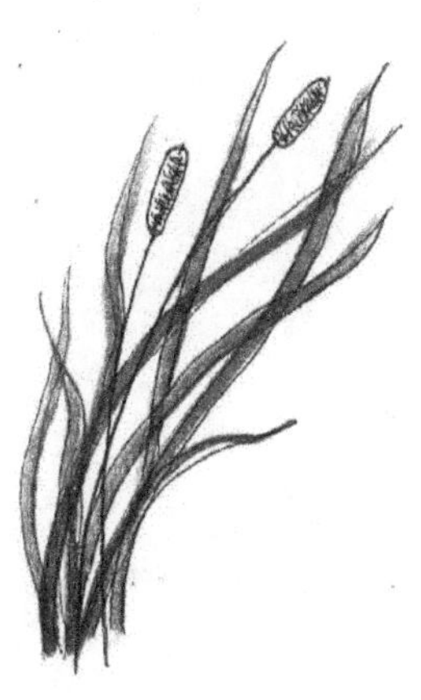

- the swans are back -

diffuse, white light on the path --
the screen door is open --
your mother is gently humming
to herself -- in the kitchen,
in the car, with the sun like wool
(so warm) -- or the *pop!* of
onions sizzling in their blue pot --
the symphony of birds --
drunken buzzing of fat yellow bees --
or the cries of kids -- the dust
dancing mid-air, caught, suspended
in late-day light -- the warmth
of shadows cast quietly in an empty
room -- or the sudden flash of
pearly white, neck extended, arched
artfully, before disappearing
into the dark and glassy blue, in search
of something good (hopefully)
-- or perhaps just some small way of
getting clean -- and i don't know
what i wanted to say, really -- except that
yesterday, amidst the bright sun,
for the first time, in such a long time --
i felt so fucking *hopeful*

- stones -

at walden pond

passing of wind through leaves
sounds like the stippling of rain.

light-dappled, this day
is like a slow-birth of sun.

clouds dissipate.

i am awake.
i am not exactly happy.

the ripples on the water's surface
are just like the folds of clothes --
your favorite sweater, rumpled
on the kitchen counter.

lilac.

i remember that.
its dull purple beauty.

or how i am rumpled too.
in front of you.
in color too.

you have said, more than once,
that i heave a heavy heart,
and i suppose you're right.

even though i think
what you really mean to say is:

that perhaps i don't need to.

that maybe, even, i choose to.

make this heart heavy,
that is.

this sunburnt heart,
plundered heart,
water-logged heart.

heart full of stones.

so, yes, maybe i carry more than i should
in this needy, knee-buckled organ.

though today, the fog lifts over the pond
like a gentle unburdening,
the day's shoulders relax.
a slow ease of blue in the sky.

and i --
as empty as the sunken lines
on my palms.

my hands are childless,
for once.

just skin, and air, and awe.

still, later, i will leave with stones,
making their familiar music
from the soft cotton insides of my pockets,
weighted down by their discordant jangle.

something to remember this moment by.
more for this tiny, mighty heart to haul
over the hill

perhaps towards you, or not -- i don’t know,
though always, eventually, finally,

towards a home i couldn't yet place,
but which bellows my name
almost every day.

michael

- café algiers (harvard sq) -

the romance of a ruined place...

i will never meet a man for coffee   at café algiers
but i think
i like it better this way, never really   knowing

left wondering...

would this man have reached for   my hand
with oceanless eyes
or proffered another small sort-of   gesture?

and afterwards...

would we have walked the slickened   streets of
cambridge together?
or flitted away for more minutes of   loneliness?

(deflated: *not the one i want, i guess)*

i like to think...

there would have been more cups of   coffee
long into the night
& records & swilling red wine from   paper cups

one fastfalling night that never really   ended
at all, and
the taste of it permanently lodged in   my mouth

like black coffee & honey...

so that when i swallow, there's the lingering taste of a
night i chose to trust in the romance of a ruined place
and in the fantasy, i realize i don't feel so ruined   anymore

- headlamp -

or, *instructions for surviving a broken heart*

i asked again, and again, and again:

what if i'm no good?
what if i'm all there ever is?
what if the man i love doesn't want me, quite?
what if the clouds just keep coming, and coming, and coming?
what if i never learn to love the right things, or let them love me back?

and then waited, and waited, and waited,
but there was no other voice,
nothing speaking me back to myself.
no better-angels.

i only ever heard my own echo
in that dark room.

i didn't like the distorted story
my echo told.

so, after a long while,
wishing for a different ending,
a softer voice which never sounded,
i took a belated breath,
put my hand out,

and fumbled forward
through that onyx black,

looking for a light.

- fried egg -

i stood in the silence of you. and then,
after, eventually, in the silence of myself.
it isn't easy. they don't tell you that --
the way the quiet cuts if you let it.

every day -- in the bathroom -- in the bed --
in the kitchen -- frying eggs, or toasting bread,
the pale light and just the suffocating silence of me.

and outside -- bird cries, a car alarm,
swaying of trees, the city awakening.

i talk to myself out loud now, sometimes,
like a friend, like the comfortingly fuzzy patter
of a portable radio, sitting on the kitchen counter.

i need you to know: *this doesn't end.*

instead, it's a new language i'm learning, every day --
how to speak as if i, too, am in the room,

and am something, someone,
beloved.

- the loneliness is part of it -

the car, the move, the acceptance letter,
the scholarship, the friday i drove away,

the light so bright that morning,
the leaves on the trees sun-dappled,

early-august, bright green
and alive with heat and color

my parent's street, where i grew up,
had lived so much of my little life

my mother teary-eyed, hugging me,
didn't leave the living room --

i couldn't look back --

the song of the city as i passed,
past mystic valley parkway,

watched as my childhood home,
forever forest-green-and-white,

fell away in the rearview mirror,
fading faintly behind me

///

and so suddenly salem

new life, new light streaming
in through alien windows

(not mine -- not yet)

and days of feeling whole, feeling fine,
of feeling like i could die, and i --

to be honest, i don't really know
which way this will go --

i don't know, i don't know,
i don't know

because good things
don't simply save us from ourselves --

or from the sound of the ticking clock
at 2:13 am --

and the bed is cold, the room is dark,
the house is still --

you are alive
and you are trying to sleep --

you are watching the vinyl clock,
its second-hand stop, tick again

jutting forward-jutting backward,
back-and-forth, again-and-again,

stuck --

trying to convince yourself
you are where you want to be,

are supposed to be --

that any of us have that certainty --
but we don't --

or i don't,
never do --

i think that's why i drive anxiously
by the coast, blaring-car-radio-blast --

i think it's why i distrust men who say
they know which way they're headed

as if this is a prize,
as if this is why they're alive --

who say what they really want is
a guy with a good head on his shoulders --

i have never had a *good head* like that,
i have never been the man who smiles

and says *i'm fine*
over bellinis, breakfast-in-bed

i'm sorry -- i am not, i may never be,
i will never be

(probably)

and so the scholarship is good,
the apartment is fine,

the sunlight is strained, though growing,
the feeling is strange --

the words are swallowed sometimes
by loneliness because you are lonely --

fuck, you are *so* lonely
sometimes –

but then again,
no man with strawberry-hair,

with soft-smile,
with a temporarily-warm-bed,

will make this feeling go away
for good,

or will fix it for you,
however much you want him to

///

because i suppose the loneliness is part of it:

it is the strain,
it is the change,

it is the small
and stupid accumulation of days

that become the simple miracle of *you* --
and your life, of what's to come,

of who you become --

it is the sing-scream of song, by the beach,
storm-on-the-horizon, the waves roiling,

the light bright and cutting,
the day unfettered,

not totally in your control,

but you screamed
back at its strange weather --

you survived it –

because you're here,
you're not exactly whole,

but you're here --
you're tired and terrified,

you're twenty-seven,
only twenty-seven,

you're too far to fail,
too smart to claim to know everything,

or *anything*
at all --

so just sing,
just drive,

just trust that to be alive
and to be kind

is enough,
has to always-be-enough --

because it is --
and you are --

and you will be --
you will be *fine* --

at least,
some of the time --

or no --

you will be more than fine –

you will live --
you will grow --

you will forget the fever of this time --

the sun will shine --
recede --

shine again --
recede again --

shine --

you will sing --
you will drive --

you will forget
you're alive --

but fuck --
you're alive.

- you have time -

you are not old.
it is not too late.

this is not a boat you missed.
things are not *once-in-a-lifetime.*

so many times in a lifetime,
we wake up to our lives.

26, 56, i don't know:

personally, i might
stumble forward
my whole life.

i could have died at 23.

(but i didn't.)

i could have chosen to be forever
numb to my life, at 24, maybe 25.

or i could have given up on a lonely
sunday in salem, sent reeling home.

(but i didn't.)

trusting time --
it's almost impossible,
i really wish it wasn't.

i wish i could go back to the me at 23
and say: *you will get up off that floor*
or *i promise, that floor is not forever.*

i wish i could go back to the me at 24,
wanting more (never sure how to get it),
and say:

*you will get it. you will work, you will wonder,
you will ask for more of your life and feel entitled
to it, but you are not entitled to it.*

(and yes, this is hard, this is a lesson,
this is, perhaps, *the* lesson.)

you will take the bit of time you have and
tend to it with your hands. like it's clay.

you will waste time, want time back, work
against the clock, and wake up the next day,
anyway.

you are not too old.
it is not too late.
you are here.
it is raining.
it is wednesday.
it is one more day
towards this great,
uncertain thing you
will make of your life.

always.
every day.
today.

- tomatoes -

after ada limón's "trying"

i've been thinking about tomatoes,
bright red on the vine,

i've been thinking about your mouth

i've been thinking about what you said then,
in that whiskey-amber-ashen cloud,
in the back of the bar, the vinyl red booth:

///

i don't know... maybe it's just enough to know
that you've grown, or you know, are growing...
**something*, however small... you know?*

then laughed at yourself, and looked away,
as if to say: *don't listen to me... i'm drunk*

///

i've been thinking about *something*
what that means, really (no, really),

and i've been thinking about the birch tree,
swaying gently outside my window

how it wants for nothing
(at least i think)

and that gentle, miraculous music of small feet,
thudding against pavement,

their surprised laughter as the cold

of the sprinkler's canon gets them good,

what a marvelous sound it is,
what a glorious world it is with them in it,

and i've been thinking about your hand in my hair,
the wind through the window of your small black car,
where we fucked for the first time

i've been thinking about the jobs i loved,
and loathed, and then left, never looked back

i've been thinking about the friends come-and-gone,
the ones sunken into my skin like the subtle gray lines
of the tattoo that's faded, although never fully

i've been thinking about that small apartment,
my first, twenty, shortly twenty-one,
that phantom version of me

so quietly culled and happy,
so uncertain about everything

how he read in parks, smoked cigarettes,
sang in the shower, loudly, mid-afternoon,
mid-august, humid, a cold water baptism
set to some stevie song

not knowing anything was ahead,
none of it,

not knowing he'd be forever further,
closer, to who he really was,
every day

all the time, all these years later, still searching,
still writing stupid little songs for sanity,

for quiet,
for creation,

still reaching out
and touching the tall white trellises,
where those ruddy, ripe tomatoes sit,

so pleasantly red,
so pleasantly plump
and imperfect,

just growing, growing,
still growing,

still

g
r
o
w
i
n
g

- at the local dive in bayou st. john -

and the bartender asks if i want another.
i peer up from my book, down at my glass,

at that thin sliver of muddled sunshine,
golden-amber and pooled, like a provocation,
there at the bottom,
and the sweat collecting
along the sensual curve of the glass,
running in thin rivulets.

i consider carefully, almost-relent,
but then say:
nah, i'm good. thanks though.

he nods, tosses the towel over his shoulder:
okay, brother.

i pause, glance around the room:

distressed blue walls
and dark wood
and stained glass

plus pin-up posters
and beer bottles
and ceiling fans
spinning lazily,
a wheeze of warm-ish air
getting pushed around the room,
no discernible relief
from the heat.

it's a wednesday.
6pm. post-work,
pre-dinner crowd.

outside, it's swamp-and-scorch hot,
a sea of late-day crescent city sun.

outside, the locals have collected,
talking and smoking and laughing
and ordering abitas
and shots
and shouting *hey marianna!*
or *chris!*
or *this fucking guy!*
to familiar faces
from down the block.

inside, the chatter and laughter
and energy in the room
is so high, it's cacophonous.

i return to the page before me –
formerly new and crisp-clean,
now slightly bent and weather-worn,
beer-and-crawfish-and-hot-sauce-stained.

i smile softly to myself,
lick my finger,
then turn the page.

i think i'm gonna be here awhile.

and as i settle into my booth,
into the bar,
into this moment of my life,

which is strange and solo,
which is languid and lonely,
which is glorious and good,

i realize, remind myself:

you have tried everything else,
so, please, do this --

take a risk on joy.

- warm -

i want to feel this warm
for the rest of my life

(even though, yes,
i know -- none of us
get such certainty,
really)

i am sitting in the sun,
on a tuesday, early morning,
neighborhood still asleep,
and from the porch,
my comfortable perch,
the lives inside are so still,
silent

no clatter of cutlery
or morning music yet --
instead, i sit, thinking,
drinking coffee, writing

mostly, i think about
my hand on your back,
which i placed gingerly
at first, then steadily,
as we ambled through
downtown newburyport,
that smile in your eyes

that way you looked at me
as we walked in tandem
with your housemate,
so quiet for a moment,
a delicious lull, and so

i looked off, very satisfied,
trying to appear pensive,
impenetrable

but then,
out of the corner of my eye,
i spied you laughing at me,
gently

i assume
because i looked a bit silly

though maybe
because i also looked
a bit beautiful, too

///

but then i also think
about that afternoon,
now many moons ago,

when i went to pride
and porchfest
with friends,
on a saturday

we drank beer,
sat on the steel lips
of a now-defunct train track,
listened to live music
and laughed loudly

god,
that day was wide
and wonderful,
sun-drenched --

a moment later,
as i stood back
to take a polaroid,
to try to capture
this moment,
its fragile magic

i could feel these
warm tears tugging
at the corners
of my eyes

and though
i was embarrassed,
i just let them go

///

i don't know,
i guess i just felt so...
warm. and connected,
you know?

i said to you later,
over a glass of white wine,
at that oyster bar,
street-side.

like i felt really alive,
in love with my life,
in that moment.

i shook my head,
thought suddenly --
why am i telling him this? –
and took a sip from my glass,
then said:

i want more moments like that. --
paused to take another drink --
shit... i... i don't know.
do you ever get those --
you know, happy tears?

and you grinned,
and were gorgeous
in the low-light,
as you replied,
with this warm,
watery glint
in your eye:

all the time.

- porch chair, pt. ii (*haiku*) -

for stevie

glass of cold amber
            against obsidian sky
and your voice a drum

- bitter/sweet (*love song*) -

embarrassed to admit this but

i think i'd
like to lie
in the quiet
of you
for just a little
longer

or maybe
instead
i'd sing you
into me
with a melody
as soft as
// summer rain //
and ask for
your hair to
take, to weave,
into mine

so that we're
one long,
unbroken
braid
together,
intertwined

just hair
on hair
on hunger
& body heat

our bodies
one endless

stream of
our ourselves
inside one
another

all brown hair
& boyish
& beautiful
blemish

until we
become
like a river
running
which is
brown
from the rust

but bitter/
sweet.

- witness(protection) -

lay with me in the soft, blue place
where the boy in you was told he
had nowhere, nowhere to go, and
i will take you/him home

and even if it doesn't last, and
one day this/us is in the past,
still, it will have been worth it:

to watch what's boyish in you
beat through the chest of the
near-carcass of what they tried
to kill in you, but they couldn't
and, yes, i'll be a witness to this

to the soft, tender animal you
are, and the arch of your body,
the pulse of what within you is
so gallant & good, like the frantic
beating of the butterfly's wings
against cupped hands, enclosed,
or like the heart that bleeds but
beats, still, in spite of everything

tender, in spite of everything
loving, in spite of everything
and beautiful (that too)

so, you should know:
even if this doesn't last,
or is left only in the past,

i'll be a witness to you
i'll be a witness to you

- august 31 -

i remember moths
at the mesh screen   nesting

and music playing distantly,
dinner's done

summer night
porch light

smell of incense,
beer

and i had you   here

held your eyes
inside mine

across the feeble flicker
of candlelight

face familiar
even in shadow

so i wondered:
what if i had this
way with you
all   my   life

and sometimes
time has this way
of breaking
like a bone

          and you watch the river
reverse

you put the beer bottle
back down on the table

or rewind the record
for even the needle knows

to change its course

you took your hand
removed your fingers
from my face

took your tongue
from inside my tongue

and put your hunger   back

i closed my mouth
i wanted to save that kiss

to cure the cancer
of *later*

when all the
moths would go

and i'd be left alone
with the scent
of a summer
that would always,
inevitably
run out

the way that summers
always do

because you

reminded me of
the way that i am
always pitched
somewhere
halfway between

wanting this moment
never-ending,
or not at all,

because to start
also means to stop,
and too soon,

means soaking
dishes in the sink
and the lonely clatter
of cutlery in the basin,
under faucet head

and the flame's
extinguished,
dessert is done
and you're gone,
all alone again

so, maybe
we're not meant
to turn the tide
of time

for you'll always
lose that battle
with *later*

and the bottle breaks,
wind picks up,

night turns cold,
record runs out,
needle stops, natch

and so, the moths
will always go

i know, *i know*
i burn candles,
anyway

i make every
nighttime shadow
into the shape of you

as i sit in the faint
auburn glow of
the porch light,
now-autumn night

in the stillness of
listening to some
stevie song

ghostly sounds from
the record player
spinning somewhere
inside

and so

i move the needle back
put your mouth
back onto my mouth

put your tongue back
inside my tongue

and now the dinner's
become undone

night rewinds

the song restarts
the song restarts

and the screen's full
of moths again

but suddenly
they're different
this time

i don't know why

or maybe it's because:
this is a different night

for we cannot try to keep
things trapped (in amber)

nothing good really lasts
or stays that way

we must tend to them
long beyond the beer
and incense

or let them go

fuck --

i know, i know, i know

i know

- untitled ii -

the day went the way
of the wine bottle:

drunk happily,
now empty.

we sat around for a while,
not really talking,
smiling softly into the blue-dark.

and i couldn't help but i wonder:

wasn't this small, uncertain pleasure,
this day spent in sensual silence together,

just our way, really, of dealing
with the idea, the inevitability,

of death?

- night writing -

and the day is lessening
the light.

it's almost out.

a candle melting down to wax.
the wick.

and it's all indigo now.

these lines -- they're slanted.
can barely see my pen.

my hand, my heart
are full of summer
and song.

and if not a poem, really,
then perhaps a prayer --

let me love my life like this,
beyond one inky august night.

amen.

- ode to dance floor -

donna summer, i think --
disco, anyway,

and those beautiful boys,
who are bathed in blue --
just the whir of m o t i o n
fingers chests eyes
toothy smiles

glancing at you
across the low-light,
the chilled glass,
the dark wood of the bar counter,
our convenient corner,

i shrugged,
sipped,
said:

one day,
i'll be less afraid,
*be like *that guy* --*

gesturing
to the piss-and-vinegar center of the room,
to a man who was only-vaguely-handsome,
much-like-me,

shirt unbuttoned sloppily,
but loose-limbed, and laughing,
shimmying, shaking e v e r y t h i n g,
under the pulsing lights,
sweaty & happy,

-- just out there, you know. doing it.

and as i caught your eye after,
which was pale blue, icy at first,
i thought maybe i had offended,
even angered you somehow --
as i sat, thinking, drinking,
from the safety of the bar stool.

but you only nodded,
then looked off, out,
into the beautiful, brazen crowd,
now crowned with confetti,
took a swig from your glass,
exhaled, turned back to me,

and –
before eventually slipping into
the delicious throng yourself,

into the thick cloud of sweat,
or the sticky-sad-sweet feeling,
which was heavy, and everywhere,
in the room,

into the softly-unclenching fist
of the dance floor,

its grime,
its glory

-- you said,
with eyes like embers,
with the most serious,
sincere smile
that you could muster:

you become the one you feed.

- cattails -

for cat

in my imagination of us,
we're here, always here --

on the boardwalk, by the brackish water,
amidst the cattails, the fruiting furry spikes,
orange-brown, and balmy breeze.

and the narrow reeds, which are summer-green,
and the open sky, and silence.

the wind picks up, your hairs on end. electricity.
and the scent of earth, alive. and nothing else.

i say: *this is my favorite thing.*
and you smile, say: *i know.*

outside, the sounds of the city rage on --
occasionally beautiful, yes, but more often
dense with pain, and discordant, and darkly-tuned.

everything is, in some sense, broken.
everything is, in some sense, waiting to be saved.
to be found beautiful or above the fray.

though at some point you say: *i'm not waiting anymore.*

which i take to mean, perhaps,
that you are already beautiful. and know it.
or are already saved, or never to be saved.

we stand there a while, warm
and watching the way the heads of the cattails sway,
softly smiling to ourselves. one another.

i ask: *what's the hardest thing you've ever done?*
and you say: *live.*

i ask: *what's the best thing you've ever done?*
and you say: *live.*

- black dog -

the black dog is imbued with magic.
she shakes her soggy coat, dark tendrils
of water shooting off her like sparks.

her smile may be misunderstood,
by some, for panting.

but this is a mistake.
she is smiling.
it is holy.

the beach behind her is imbued with magic
too.

the waves, the water, roil and roll
over the patiently-waiting sand
as though nothing has happened.

the ocean does not know it is 2022.

the creamy shells,
which litter this nearly-empty beach,
are mere shards.

they do not know it is 2022 either.
they only know to be curved and ragged
and sharply beautiful.

the old man who whistles for the black dog
is imbued with magic too.

he has his forehead pressed into his hands.
he must know it is 2022.

but when he lifts his wrinkled face
from the wizened cup of his palms,
there is no sorrow there.

or, at the very least,
nothing as simple as sorrow.

the man touches the sand, the smooth stones,
calls the black dog in the voice of the very beloved,
and then is off -- down the beach, ever further away,
into the world, the extinguishing day,

the gently blackening sky.

- margins / last page -

i don't know
if this is the last thing i'll write
here.

for there are still margins
in the pages
of this book

and places to revise,
to mark and meddle
and scratch out.

the lined-page-as-scorched-earth.

and i was thinking
earlier today:

my life is in the margins,
is the margins,

for i am always
anywhere -- or nowhere --

at all,

rewriting my mind,
my tongue, for later.

though i never seem to change,
truly.

///

and so, surprise-surprise:

i'm sitting on my porch
on a summer night
writing (attempting to).

and the blazing orange shadows
have already left the backs of the houses
behind mine mere moments ago.

it is sunday. it is quiet.
just the rustle of emerald leaves
and the rusty creak of the screen door latch
and the occasional car whizzing past.

and i was nearly-dead with sorrow
just days ago
(and still am, i suppose).

though tonight, the neighbor's baby
slurs a very happy
hello! hello!
from the porch below --

first for his happily-captive parents,
then to the birds, the trees,
the wilting flowers,
for a half-an-hour straight.

i listen for his grown-ups' laughter,
rising up over the branches
of the sycamores,
through the thin gray slats
of the porch railing, over to me,
inside the fabric of my clothes,
inside my bones.

///

most days, i am in the margins,
pale white and wonder --
yet underneath,
neon-bright, pulsing
with grief, and guilt,
and good intentions,
wanting everything
(wanting nothing).

most days,
i forget who i am
and then remember,
temporarily
(and then forget again).

most days,
i write, then rewrite,
the lines of my life

before closing the journal,
inhaling, exhaling deeply

and gently swaying to some song
you've probably heard before
but had forgotten the words,
or the melody, until now,

until i wrote you, to remind you,
to tell you of my life
(and your life, too, i suppose):

its often-awful, impossible arc,
its on-and-on-and-on-and-on,

its indelible music.

bonus tracks

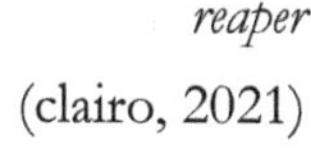

reaper

(clairo, 2021)

***

i'm down, whatever

(jw francis, 2020)

***

this is how we walk on the moon

(arthur russell, 1994)

***

out loud

(remember sports, 2021)

***

hold on

(alabama shakes, 2012)

***

summer girl

(haim, 2020)

• acknowledgements •

i wrote the majority of this collection at a moment in my life when i was at my gloomiest, lowest, loneliest, winteriest. the idea of summer, of endlessly unfurling august nights, felt so perfect and unattainable. in truth, at that time, i wasn't sure i'd make it to another summer.

thank you to the folks who helped me limp, then walk, and eventually stride along to another june, july, august.

to my beautiful parents, always. to my sister, who is endlessly kind.

to my aca coworkers, who are as much my family as they are my friends.

to the men i got the chance to love these past few years – however imperfectly and even when it hurt. i don't know if i trust the old adage that says *"what doesn't kill you makes you stronger"* -- but i do believe that the heart is a muscle that we can choose to either exercise or neglect. i feel lucky that, in these past few years, i got a lot of exercise. my heart is sore, though stronger too.

and lastly, to my friends, the loves of my life – chief among them, skye, my best friend and eternal prom date. and cat, the ernie to my bert, my once-upon-a-time coworker and roomie and beard and platonic life partner.

these love songs are for you all.

• about our press •

About Pumpkin Boy Press

Pumpkin Boy Press is an independent publishing press, founded by aspiring writer Michael Mahin in 2021. Pumpkin Boy Press prioritizes queer voices and queer stories, especially of the spooky & sparkly & sad & sweet variety. You can learn more about us at: **www.pumpkinboypress.com**

••

About the Author

Michael Mahin is a poet, book designer, and educator, currently based in Arlington, Massachusetts. He is also queer and a recent cancer survivor. You can contact Michael at: **pumpkinboypress@gmail.com**

••

About the Illustrator

Cat Beaudoin produces celebratory art and creative spaces through her multidisciplinary work in visual arts, community, and education. Informed by thoughtful moments in nature, arts-oriented spaces for learning, and a deep curiosity of sharing culture, Cat's work honors the diverse beauty of our world. Cat's accentuation of color in her subjects as well as her emphasis of expression and understanding in her facilitation highlight an eagerness to expand consciousness in moments big and small. You can learn more about Cat and their artwork at **www.catbeaudoinart.com** and on Instagram at **@catbeaudoinart**.

• songs for "summer nights" •

---

so much, if not all, of my writing is inspired by music. for this collection, it was the music of long, languid, occasionally-lonely, sometimes-libidinous summer nights.

songs for wine, for wandering, for porch sitting, for parks, for protracted sunsets, for swimming.

for dusk, for dinner, for the dance floor.
for sex. for sweat. for cicadas. for silence.

as such, i have curated a lil playlist of summer songs, which compelled the writing; some are explicitly referenced in the preceding poems, others just capture that unique june/july/august-at-dusk kinda vibe.

to be listened to while drinking a glass of white wine on some hot, horny, holy summer night – or, you know, while merely dreaming of one.

enjoy.

scan the QR code below to listen to the "songs for summer nights" playlist on Spotify, or visit: ***tinyurl.com/songs4summernights***

Printed in the USA
CPSIA information can be obtained
at www.ICGtesting.com
JSHW021917311024
72797JS00004B/14